BRITISH RAILWAY DIESEL MEMORIES

No. 64: 'D' FOR DIESELS :

DAVID DUNN

ISBN 978-1-909625-02-0

INTRODUCTION

Welcome to Volume 5 of D for Diesels. Once again we have an eclectic mix of illustrations from all parts of the UK – well nearly everywhere – which we hope you will find not just interesting but factual too with explanatory captions written to enlighten and hopefully amuse in some cases.

It is always difficult to choose what goes into each volume because the material is such that everything wants to be in there now without having to wait for the next volume to arrive. Actually it is nice to have such a wealth of illustrations. So, no complaints from me!

Besides being on shed, in stations, and on works too, we have really ventured out onto the main line this time with some unusual images at places 'off the beaten track' along with some nice comparison views of various classes to help modellers 'get it right!'

We finish off the selection of each volume with images depicting diesels in trouble but this time we illustrate two serious incidents, which not only had fatal consequences for passengers but also for the locomotives involved. They are sobering because no matter how many safety precautions are implemented, something out of the ordinary can arise to threaten even the best laid plans.

Finally, we would like to thank the Armstrong Railway Photographic Trust (ARPT) for the use of images herein.

Cover (*see opposite*)

Title page **The return, Up empties, working of the Cliffe-Uddingston cement train passing York's Holgate platform at an unknown date in 1962 with D6578 leading an unidentified member of the class (see also later). Did anyone ever photograph this train with a single Type 3 in charge?** *K.Linford (ARPT).*

Printed and bound by The Amadeus Press, Cleckheaton, West Yorkshire
First published in the United Kingdom by Book Law Publications, 382 Carlton Hill, Nottingham, NG4 1JA

D0280 FALCON reverses out of King's Cross termini on 16th August 1962. This handsome prototype diesel electric locomotive first arrived on the Eastern Region on 13th October 1961 to commence trials on the ECML from Finsbury Park. A regular working in 1962 was the *MASTER CUTLER* Pullman from Sheffield (Victoria). Powered by two high-speed Maybach engines, and named after its birthplace Falcon works at Loughborough, the prototype had quite a productive, though not an easy life, and was eventually purchased by BR for £20,000 in December 1970. Renumbered D1200 – the 0280 number was concocted from the fact it was the 280th diesel locomotive built by Brush – the Co-Co was given the overall Rail blue livery. It was distinctive in being the only 'trial' prototype acquired by BR. The livery here was lime green with an olive green band around the lower body. The buffer beams were a shade of orange whilst the name was painted in black on a light blue Falcon silhouette above which was the stainless steel cast falcon. Besides trials on the ER, D0280 took part in one-off tests during the early months of 1962 such as the haulage – Including stop and starts – of lengthy trains of passenger stock (up to 22 carriages), and, later, mineral wagons on the Lickey incline, with and without banking assistance. Just weeks after this scene was recorded it was working coal trains in the East Midlands, allocated to the temporary diesel depot at Shirebrook West (the converted goods shed pre-dating the purpose built depot). Although the Maybach engines were not to BR's liking (similar units however powered the 'Western' class for instance and were the preferred prime movers in WR traction thinking) the lightweight body design, known as the Hirondelle Truss, was favoured and was used by Brush for the D1500 Type 4 class. FALCON ended its days on the Western Region, at Ebbw Junction, and was finally withdrawn in October 1975 after a 'trial' withdrawal in May 1974 only to be re-instated a month later. Unserviceable by the summer of 1975 with traction motor failure, the inevitable took place exactly fourteen years (to the day I wonder?) after coming onto BR property to show its paces. *D.J.Dippie.*

3

Fresh from a heavy overhaul and wearing the BR Brunswick or Locomotive Green livery, 'Warship' D833 PANTHER graces the yard at Swindon works on the south side of 'A' shop. It is Sunday 19th September 1965, and since leaving the paint shop some days beforehand, the B-B has done some road testing, the tell-tale dirt having already stained the lower body and black painted bogies. However, the rest of the paintwork is still looking pristine and that is how Newton Abbot depot will receive their charge when Swindon decided to put it back into traffic. Note that D833 is adorned with the BR crest above the nameplate, which was normal, and the light grey mid-drift body cheatline extends between the cab doors. The yellow warning panel on the ends had appeared in 1962 and had quickly become a standard feature - the full yellow ends were first applied from March 1967. By this stage in its life, the five-year old locomotive was one of those working the Waterloo-Salisbury-Exeter passenger services; not only because the Southern Region had nothing suitable in their diesel stable to replace the Bulleid Pacifics, but the 'Warships had become semi-surplus on their native Western Region with the introduction of the 'Westerns' and the Brush Type 4s. Unable to compete with the latter two classes, singly, on the fastest timings of the heavier passenger trains on the WR, the 'Warships were successfully run, double-headed, towards the end of the decade. This was in order to speed up some of the principal West of England expresses. By 1965 most of the class were allocated to Newton Abbot depot but Laira still had a reasonable number shedded there. *K.Groundwater (ARPT).*

On that same Sunday at Swindon works, D833 was joined on its siding by sister D857 UNDAUNTED which had not yet had any road testing as the maroon livery is immaculate all the way down to the bottom of the skirt. This was D857's first application of the maroon livery which was first used from 1964. Note the BR crest has been replaced by one of the coaching stock ciphers which tended to show up better on the maroon paint (these circular 'badges' were used on many contractor-built classes when locomotives were first introduced but they fell out of favour on other regions and were replaced at the first major overhauls by crests). The cheatline is also omitted with this livery change and the nameplate background paint was changed from red to black; all the small touches of the original style were being eliminated even by 1965 as the move towards the 'plain Jane' Rail blue got underway. On this date D857 was apparently allocated to Newton Abbot too but the shed plate affixed to the front end of the solebar clearly displays 84A – Laira! Both locomotives managed to keep their North British builders plates and they have been carefully masked during painting. From early days the B-B 'Warships' became daily visitors to Crewe, working throughout from the West Country on both passenger and freight services. On certain Sunday's in the early Sixties' it was possible to find three of them stabled on Crewe North shed, a couple on Crewe South shed, and one or two languishing for the weekend on the siding above Gresty Lane shed! They made quite a change from the noisy, lumbering English Electric Type 4s, although the 'Warships' rarely appeared in a condition such as depicted here. *K.Groundwater (ARPT)*.

Staying at Swindon on that September Sunday in 1965, we enter 'A' shop where one of the original A1A-A1A 'Warships' D603 CONQUEST (*above*) is up on stands whilst the fitters who struggle to make the thing work properly had a day off. These were the 'bad boys' of the hydraulic world and the WR tried everything possible to get them working as per specification but to no avail. This must have been one of D603's last visits to Swindon shops because just over two years later, along with the rest of it small band of sisters, it was withdrawn (after months of idleness) and sold for scrap. Their home depot was Laira where the then fairly new and modern facilities included overhead cranes of ample capacity to lift the engines and gearboxes out of these locomotives. Such facility would render visits to Swindon to something of a rarity but that was never the case (Newton Abbot was similarly equipped) and for some reason the draw of a main works trip to Swindon was deemed as a necessity; surely a waste when Laira was so generously endowed. (*left*) One of the scrap bins containing some of the discarded plumbing and wiring from inside D603! *K.Groundwater (ARPT).*

PANTHER once again, and at Swindon! Although undated, this photograph probably depicts the time when the diesel was first given the yellow warning panel application from 1962 onwards, the painters stands and planks being erected at both ends of the locomotive. New to Laira on 6th July 1960, D833 went to Newton Abbot on 12th August 1961 in one of the early groups to establish the class at that depot. At the end of July 1967 it was transferred to Old Oak Common for a three year stint before returning to Devon. Shortly after its arrival in London the 'Warship' was loaned to Bescot depot for three weeks during August. Withdrawn on 3rd October 1971, D833 was cut up at Swindon during the first month of 1972. Now then, it will be noticed that PANTHER has been renumbered to D333 during the course of its time in the shops; not only was the renumbering done at this end, it was also done at the other end too – a profession job by any standard – but it is unknown if the other side of the locomotive was so treated. Nevertheless a wag was at work within the confines of Swindon! I wonder if any locomotives managed to get out onto the road before the petty vandalism was spotted. Did you ever see or photograph such practical jokes? *K.H.Cockerill (ARPT)*.

(*above and below*) The Sunday line-up of diesel shunters outside the amenities block, at Corkerhill depot on 17th May 1964! Locomotives on view but not in any order are: D2438, D2440, D3922, D3923, and D3924. Although they had different types of power transmission, they all had one thing in common – the filth. *Both A.Ives (ARPT).*

Making a nice pleasant change to the previous illustrations we present this ten years old, and obviously ex-works, Drewry 0-6-0DM which was stabled at Carlisle Kingmoor depot on Sunday 7th May 1967. Not many of the class got this far north but D2253 had been sent to Carlisle (transfer date week ending 6th May 1967) from Derby for reasons unknown. It wasn't resident at 12A for too long and was transferred to Speke Junction seven months later on 6th January 1968. Originally numbered 11223, the diesel-mechanical had started life on the Southern Region at Hither Green on 10th April 1957 – one of ten Robert Stephenson & Hawthorn built examples (11220–11229) sent new to the SR in 1957. Nearly ten years to the day-ish (4th February 1967) D2253 was transferred away from the SR to the LMR and ended up at Derby. It appears from the time frame that 17A sent it into works shortly after arrival at Derby and once released it was then transferred to Kingmoor in this pristine condition; how nice! Renumbered in May 1961 during an overhaul at Eastleigh, the little 0-6-0 worked at various depots on the SR including Ashford and Stewarts Lane but always managed to return to Hither Green. It was the only one of its nine peers which left the SR and being part of the non-standard Class 04 when TOPS was introduced, it was withdrawn from Allerton depot in March 1969 as D2253 and later sold. *A.Ives (ARPT).*

Returning to the realities of BR's diesel fleet in its normal condition, we find one of the original 'Peaks' D4 GREAT GABLE, stabled at its home depot Toton, on Sunday 1st May 1966. Sister D6 is buffered up at the No.1 end whilst at this end is an ex-works but unidentified member of the class. Nothing remarkable so far but lets look at the illustration in detail: Graffiti; plenty of it on this beast and worth emulating on any model if you are so inclined. Dirt; likewise but still not very often presented on models at any scale - do railway modellers have more respect for their models than BR did for its locomotives? Fittings; firstly, I'm going to stick my neck out and state that D4 was the only member of the class so fitted! What? Both nose ventilation grills have what appear to be rectangular frames stuck on as an afterthought. The same grills also have carefully cut rectangular recesses in their lower halves. Just below them, the body skirt has a small foot hole cut out, and just below those are two footsteps fixed onto the bogie, two-thirds up and bottom. So, we are looking at a means of crew men be able to reach the front windows in order to clean them prior to the locomotive getting underway. The aforementioned frames were two hand rails partly incorporated into the frame of the ventilation grill. The final extra fitting was the hand grip on the top of the nose whereby someone can hold on with one hand and both feet in the ventilator recess whilst administering a cloth to the window. Photographic evidence has shown that D4 was the only Class 44 'Peak' to get these adornments and they were only fitted on this side of the locomotive so that the driver had clear vision when No.1 end was leading whilst the secondman had the same when No.2 end was leading! Unlike the English Electric Type 4s built at the same time, BR failed to see the usefulness of the hatches in the top of the nose compartment and therefore cleaning front windows was always a problem. The experiment/trial was not proceeded with any further it seems so D4, in its own little way, was quite unique amongst its brethren. *A.Ives (ARPT)*.

We never fail to include one of the Scottish Region NBL Type 2s in this series and for starters in this album we include D6112 standing forlornly (they usually were) and out on a limb at St Rollox depot on Saturday 16th May 1964. Discarded, dumped, rejected? For once the external appearance of the Bo-Bo doesn't look too bad; no scorched patches, missing or damaged panels, heavy accumulations of leaking oil. However, it does have the air of a neglected and perhaps unwanted nuisance; certain external parts are missing such as windscreen wipers so goodness knows what internal bits were missing. The open gangway doors in the nose give us a slight glimpse into the concertina connections of the gangway folded neatly – still – Inside the compartment. A rope/cable is draped over the body above the No.2 end bogie as if it is holding the locomotive together. This particular Type 2 had been stored here for some time (two years already) and would remain at this location for another two years before a desperate Scottish Region virtually rebuilt it in July 1966 from the original Class 21 standard to a newly created Class 29. The troublesome MAN engine was changed for a more powerful Paxman type but even that radical solution did little to prolong the life – and reputation – of the class so that by the end of 1971 all of the Type 2s diesel-electrics from the NBL stable had already been broken up or condemned (four of the NBL Type 2 diesel-hydraulics on the Western Region clung on until January 1972). After a further six months stored unserviceable, D6112 was condemned in December 1971 and cut up at Glasgow works during the following June – good riddance!? A.Ives (ARPT).

A more reliable locomotive type altogether! English Electric Type 1 D8089 is stabled at Kipps shed on Sunday 17th May 1964 and is one of a batch of nearly fifty of her type received brand new by Eastfield depot in the early 1960s. *A.Ives (ARPT)*.

What's this then? A Deltic without a train, yet showing ECML reporting number 1A16! The location is Durham station on 4th May 1963 and the Gateshead Type 5, which was three weeks shy of its second birthday, looks decidedly grubby in the 52A tradition. However, mucky they might have been at Gateshead but they were usually reliable but then this was a Deltic and reliability, though high at times, took a bit of a knock whenever failures occurred whilst hauling important ECML expresses, and that was always (the haulage, not the failures). So, for this class there was no hiding in the anonymity of numbers. There were just twenty-two of them; big, brash, noisy, powerful and arrogant; the superlatives are endless. One blip and everybody saw or felt the repercussions. Note that the regimental name has yet to be affixed; when it had during the following October, the locomotive would be even more conspicuous, if that was possible. *A.Ives (ARPT)*.

The Up service of *THE MAYFLOWER* hauled by 'Warship' D601 ARK ROYAL runs into platform 7 at Taunton during the summer of 1958. This named train was inaugurated by British Railways on Tuesday 17th June 1957 and ran between Plymouth (North Road) and London (Paddington). D601 created a little bit of history for itself on Monday 16th June 1958 when it hauled the first diesel powered Down service of the long established – 1st July 1904 – *CORNISH RIVIERA EXPRESS* from Paddington to Penzance. So, that was the good news regarding this class. *R.F.Payne (ARPT).*

14

Passing beneath Bishops Road bridge, whilst making its way out of platform 10 at Paddington, on an unknown date in the 1960s, 'Western' D1068 WESTERN RELIANCE runs past the Paddington Arrivals signal box. Assuming D1068 was only requiring fuel and servicing prior to its next duty, it was possible for the C-C to proceed directly from this location to Ranelagh Bridge locomotive yard on the Down side of the main line without any reversing manoeuvres. The yard's position just outside the terminal drastically cut down on light engine movements to and from Old Oak Common depot. *Trevor Ermel.*

15

Gateshead's 350 h.p. 0-6-0DE D3316 stands in a seemingly precarious position at the peak of the incline known as Walbridge Bank Top in County Durham, June 1966. *E.Wilson (ARPT)*.

Remember the illustration on page 27 in *D for Diesels 3* featuring D2700 in the works yard at Darlington in June 1963 looking just about ready for scrapping? Well here it is nine years earlier on 12th June 1954 in the condition as received by BR from the makers NBL twelve months earlier. The contemporary finish – style and livery – give it a purposeful look but beneath that exterior lay a jar of worms waiting to give so much grief to the fitters who were given the task of looking after and maintaining the tricky little four-coupled diesel-hydraulic. Since new the 0-4-0DH had worked from West Hartlepool shed and the cleanliness of the bodywork is to be complemented. However, here it is at Darlington on one of its all-too regular visits to repair some internal problem which affected it all of its ten years life. Desperate to enter the emerging diesel locomotive market, North British Locomotive Co. had a lot to answer for when it came to their diesel designs, hydraulic or electric – their steam locomotives were superb and world beating – which mixed old and new but unproved technology. D2700 née 11700, was typical of that monumental gaff. *I.Falcus.*

On a bright, yet damp, Tuesday 2nd February 1960, EE Type 4 D252 heads south through Monkwearmouth station with a crew training trip from York. Barely six weeks old at that time, D252's cab must have seemed like something out of science fiction to the drivers who were more used to the noisy, hot/cold, and rocking footplate of steam locomotives. These training runs were much like a circular tour and certainly took in the sights: north along the ECML to Gateshead, taking the right fork and passing the motive power depot at 52A, on towards Boldon, south to Sunderland, Hartlepool, Stockton, then on to Northallerton to rejoin the ECML and a quick burst home to York. Besides the architecture, note the generous 'six-foot' through the 1848-built station. This passenger facility was closed in March 1967 by which time D252 was still a member of the 50A allocation. *D.J.Dippie.*

Another crew training run, or a locomotive test? We are on a similar route to the previously illustrated image, as D201 pauses at Eaglescliffe on an unknown date – possibly in 1958 – when Doncaster took these locomotives on acceptance runs when they were ex-manufacturers. Note that the five-coach formation has a brake at each end. *K.H.Cockerill (ARPT)*.

On a typically damp and murky day in Manchester – it was 3rd November 1963 – a chance meeting of a pair of brand new Hymeks' outside their birthplace at Gorton Foundry, and a passing train, resulted in these two rare illustrations of Beyer, Peacock products in the siding alongside the company premises (*above*). Obviously out of numerical sequence, the late delivered D7080 and on time D7092 were not in fact coupled together. It is a Sunday so the B-Bs would have spent the weekend here. (*below*) Note the tank wagons from which the all important diesel fuel was transferred to enable the locomotives to eventually make their way to their new homes on the Western Region. In the left background is the erecting shop where the pair were constructed. *Both A.Ives (ARPT).*

Staying in Manchester, we visit Newton Heath on Sunday 3rd July 1966. The first thing we see as we arrive on the premises is this Western Lines allocated Brush type 4 which had been on a crew training trip and has now stabled for the weekend outside the repair shop. Although no main line diesel locomotives were ever allocated to Newton Heath – a few dozen shunters which once called 26A home, were transferred to Longsight (on paper) at about this time to tidy up the books – the depot saw quite a number serviced and stabled at the shed. Steam was still very much in evidence at this place and would be for a couple of years yet but none of them were visible from this vantage point; the remaining section of the old steam shed was out of sight behind the new diesel multiple unit shed whose single pitched roof dominates the background of this image. Besides the 'locally based' LMR diesels from Longsight, Crewe, and Wigan being regular visitors, others came daily from Gateshead, Healey Mills, Holbeck, Neville Hill, Immingham, Kingmoor, and even further afield. *A.Ives (ARPT).*

Does this count in the D for D scheme? It was a diesel after all and its identity – stretching the parameters a bit – started with the letter D as in Departmental Locomotive No.84. Its inclusion was merited by the fabulous lining adorning the body sides and cab. This is York – I'm not quite sure where in the city – on Saturday 28th February 1959 as this brand new Ruston & Hornsby 88 b.h.p. 0-4-0DM (or was it a 2-2-0) product was proudly paraded in front of the photographers by its seemingly happy driver. The chain driven shunter is passing an old and by now redundant coaling stage used by one of its forebears but now long forgotten about by the man in the peaked cap. *N.W.Skinner (ARPT).*

In the days before the Selby Diversion was created to allow coal mining beneath the old ECML north of the town, the junction was a very busy piece of railway and something of a bottleneck with its swing bridge too. On a dull and wet Wednesday 13th June 1962, one of the daily cement trains which ran between the Blue Circle Cement plant at Cliffe, in Kent and Uddingston, Glasgow was photographed making good progress through the station with the, by now, regular motive power in the shape of two Southern Region BRC&W Type 3s. Today's pair was D6547 and D6563, both from Hither Green. It was regarded as something of a long working which departed from Cliffe just after 2 a.m. with precision timing and *eventually* very reliable locomotives with crew changes en route. Initially when the SR diesels took on the service, only one locomotive was employed but after quite a few failures it was deemed sensible to diagram a pair of the Type 3s. However, even after this picture was captured on film the, the service reverted to a single unit with dire consequences during August with numerous failures on the GN main line; why the reversion to one locomotive was authorised is unknown but perhaps summer traffic levels on the SR required that extra Type 3 for their own use. York was the furthest north that the SR engines worked to be replaced by a single (maid-of-all-work) EE Type 4 which took the heavy train on to Glasgow. The Down train usually passed Selby after midday. *I.S.Carr (ARPT).* 23

An LMS design, which was adopted by BR, is represented here by No.12120 one of ten 350 h.p. 0-6-0 DE shunters – 12113 to 12122 – delivered new from Darlington works to Dairycoates shed between 9th July and 24th September 1952. The class consisted 106 locomotives in all (12033 to 12138) which were delivered between April 1945 and December 1952 although only the first ten were actually LMS built. Detail differences meant that the class was not quite to the same specification as the ubiquitous 13XXX 0-6-0DE shunters which eventually became Class 08, therefore, under TOPS classification, they became Class 11; the '08' started to appear just as construction of Class 11 was coming to a close. None ever carried the 11 prefix and none ever got the 'D' prefix either, which means some might question their inclusion in this series. However, the ancestry of some of the important classes is worth looking at in detail if only to show the evolution and on-going modifications – no matter how subtle – metered out with each new batch of these iconic shunters. Of the Dairycoates engines, three transferred to Alexandra Dock shed in late November 1953, to be followed by another five on 13th May 1954 and finally by the remaining pair on 13th February 1955. Their place at Dairycoates being taken by new Class 08s from the D30XX, D31XX and D32XX batches, all Darlington built; in reality the ten Alex Dock engines visited 53A for maintenance throughout their time at the sub shed. They all returned (on paper) to Dairycoates when Alexandra Dock shed was closed but in reality they remained stabled within the docks complex and simply returned to the parent shed for maintenance and repair as had been the arrangement beforehand. Prior to that transfer to the docks, No.12120 was recorded at Springhead in 1953, sporting local Pilot number 78; which included working the Carriage & Wagon Dept. yard at Springhead, Monday to Friday, 0700-1800, and, at the end of each shift, moving wagons of locomotive coal into the Springhead coal stage storage. Note the slight damage to the running plate above the middle and rear wheels. 12120 was withdrawn from Dairycoates on 28th December 1968 but was then sold to the National Coal Board for further work in County Durham where it was employed for another ten years before being cut up in March 1980. It might be worth recalling that two of the Hull batch went 'on loan' to Lees shed on the outskirts of Oldham in 1956: 12113 from 28th January to 25th February, and 12115 from 25th February to 24th March. The reason for the loan so far from home, and to the LM Region to boot, was to employ them working repair trains in the Standedge tunnels which, at that time, were under the control of the NE Region Civil Engineer. *R.F.Payne (ARPT).*

So, why is this shunter included within the compilation? The ex-LMS/EE jackshaft 0-6-0DE was originally numbered, when built in March 1942, in the War Department series as WD 64. Its LMS number was 7115 but this was not applied until the 0-6-0 had left WD service in May 1942. Toton was the first depot to have its services and 18A received WD 64 straight from the works at Derby on 11th March 1942. If it ever took up employment with the WD is unknown but two months after being put into service it was transferred to Kingmoor where it remained until re-allocated to Speke Junction on 16th December 1950 as 12028. This illustration was captured at Workington at a date unknown but obviously after 1957 when the BR crest was introduced but not too many years afterwards because the adjacent diesel-shunter is wearing the old BR emblem. The why and when of 12028's stint at Workington is unknown, it may well have been on loan (such events sometimes failed to make the official record) so we can only speculate. The presence of a sister engine errs to the facts that it was not a 'one-off'. Nevertheless, 12028 qualifies for the D for D status inasmuch that it did, at one time, carry a 'D' to prefix its fleet number; scraping the barrel? You decide. It is nice to look at though, and it is ex-works clean too. *P.J.Robinson.*

On delivery to Heaton shed, Drewry 0-6-0DMs D2048 and D2047 take the by-pass line at Newcastle Central on Saturday 3rd January 1959. Ex Doncaster, the pair now wear the latest green livery and must have brightened up an otherwise dull winter Saturday for any enthusiasts following their progress. Note that a driver is inside each locomotive cab. How the pair got to Tyneside is unknown but if the Darlington 0-6-0DE delivery method was anything to go by, they must have travelled as far as Gateshead in a train where they were probably commissioned prior to letting them loose on the road. However, later deliveries of the same class of shunters from contractors works were undertaken by the locomotives themselves – see D for Diesels 3, page 31. Records show that D2047 was released from Doncaster on Friday 19th December 1958 whilst D2048 was turned out on Tuesday 23rd December. Slow progress, assuming they went by train, but it was the Christmas period with expected disruption all over the system. Still they made it. *H.Forster.*

Two views of the traverser outside the main erecting shops at Crewe works. It is an unknown date but possibly 1966 when the works was still building the Brush Type 4s of which a body shell is visible at the north end of the traverser in the upper view. (*above*) Looking north-east, with the sun in the west, a clutch of main line locomotives are undergoing last minute testing, and touch-up painting, prior to release to traffic. This group represent nearly all the classes which Crewe dealt with at that period; only the EE Type 3 is conspicuous by its absence but there would have been some around the works. There are no electric locomotives in view either but they were handled in a different section of the shops. (*below*) Looking south-east across the pit, at the same line-up which included the following: D313, D1683, D1529, D399, D8008, D1545, D360. *Both V.Wake (ARPT).*

(*opposite, top*) Darlington built BR Sulzer Type 2s D5105, on the left, and D5099, go through testing procedures at Darlington Works Crossing circa late August 1960. Though the Bo-Bos were constructed just three months apart – D5099 to traffic 3rd June, D5105 to traffic 10th September – they clearly have different 'finishes' to the paint schemes, especially the roofs. D5099's lower body dirt comes from nearly three months in traffic from Gateshead but the roof definitely is a different colour from its sister's on the left. D5099 appears to be having remedial tests - failures in traffic for new diesels was no rarity in those early years - whilst D5105 is basically complete, and also allocated to 52A, it just requires the electrical tests to prove its road worthiness. Note that both diesels have their No.2 ends to the camera. (*opposite, bottom*) The other sides of the pair, showing no change in the aforementioned panel. Darlington was one of those workshops which was a pleasure to visit (they were all good really), the rambling layout and hidden corners revealing gems like this, and the exercise was good especially, if you had walked from the station too! *Both J.W.Armstrong (ARPT).*

(*above*) This illustration of Type 2 D5046 at Stratford diesel depot on 17th August 1962 is included to show the body panel differences between itself and those on D5099 and D5105 in the previous illustration. D5046 was a product of Crewe and was put into traffic on 29th October 1959, working initially from March depot – just under a year before the other pair entered traffic – and then from Stratford from 29th September 1960. By August 1962 the Bo-Bo had transferred to Ipswich and has acquired the yellow warning panel at each end – it looks suspiciously fresh, just like the body paintwork! Now, take a look at the first ventilator panel of the lower row immediately after the built-in ladder, then look at D5105 et al. That square panel has now become a triangular panel and has increased in size by perhaps 50% – man made evolution at work! *D.J.Dippie.* 29

Out on the road now, we look at a couple of locations in the North Eastern Region. Firstly we have EE Type 4 D246 heading south through Relly Mill, past Dearness Valley signal box, circa 1960 with a diverted ECML express. The train would work through Bishop Auckland, and Shildon to regain its main line path at Darlington. *I.S.Carr (ARPT).*

Another ECML diversion, this one on Sunday 4th September 1960! Winding its way through the rather torturous layout around Bishop Auckland, EE Type 4 D274 brings a train of mainly ex-LMS coaching stock – probably a Newcastle-Liverpool – beneath a magnificent signal gantry which can also be described as 'busy.' The damp rails are no doubt helping to keep the flange squeal to a minimum. D274 was only four months old when this scene was recorded but it was a Gateshead engine hence the build-up of muck. *I.S.Carr (ARPT).* 31

D5700 in store at Derby shed on 7th May 1961. At the time the whole class of twenty locomotives were 'stored', although dumped might be a better description of the forced retirement metered out. Besides Derby, Trafford Park shed was a temporary dump/home to six of the class – D5701-04, D5710-11 – during the storage period, which lasted for about a year until the manufacturers had 'sorted out' the problems associated with the engines, etc. Note the connecting door has been left open to the elements, as had all the others; another sign of the contempt held by railwaymen for the Co-Bos. However, this image gives us a chance to study the flexible connecting tunnel poking out of D5700's nose. I wonder what the more rotund drivers thought of that short tunnel. Finally, it might be noted that the BR crest at this, the No.2, end is one of the right-facing and therefore incorrect examples. *I.H.B.Lewis.*

With the gangways connected for inter-locomotive access, BRC&W Type 2s D5312 and D5313 enter Edinburgh (Waverley) with empty stock from Graigentinny carriage sidings on Thursday 25th July 1963. For how long the practice of allowing crews to pass between locomotives went on is unknown to this compiler but illustrations showing the connections 'in action' are comparatively rare. These two Bo-Bos were part of the initial batch of twenty which went new to the southern end of the Great Northern main line, working initially from Hornsey depot and later from Finsbury Park. They were at the latter depot for only a short period because all twenty were transferred to Scottish Region and Haymarket in particular during the early summer of 1960 (this was one lot of Type 2s ScR didn't mind acquiring). It will be noted that unlike their Scottish cousins – D5320 onwards – they were not equipped with the cab recess to hold the tablet exchange equipment required for single line working. This omission basically kept them working in the lowlands and central belt of Scotland rather than the Highlands but D5316 to D5319 were transferred to Inverness at different periods during the 60s' and for that move St Rollox works fitted the necessary recesses and apparatus. D5300 to D5315 were however later equipped for working some of the first Merry-Go-Round (MGR) coal trains to run in Britain. *A.Ives (ARPT)*.

Working a 'stopper' from Dumfries on Thursday 11th April 1968, Eastfield Type 2 D5354 is photographed departing from Kirkconnel station and heading north on the former G&SWR main line in Dumfriesshire. In the background a BR Sulzer Type 2 is marshalling a train of mineral wagons ready to shunt the sidings of Fauldhead Colliery on the left of the picture. The colliery, which once had a workforce of more than 1,100 men, was sunk in 1896 and since Vesting day in 1947 had averaged an annual output of 260,000 tons of saleable coal. However, in 1968 production had ceased and the pit was closed taking another little bit of traffic away from BR. The railway station here opened much earlier than the mine and was operating in time for the line's opening in 1850. Happily, the station is still open for business and it retains a siding on the Down side. *John Boyes (ARPT).*

One of the 'early' batch fitted for single line working was D5319 which is seen on Tuesday 1st October 1968 working a rather short pick-up freight on the Speyside line in Morayshire. Having just left Grantown-on-Spey, the Type 2 is en route from Aviemore to Craigellachie. This particular locomotive worked from both Haymarket and Inverness during the decade, its first move to Inverness being on 7th April 1962. On 23rd October 1965 it was back to Edinburgh for a fourteen month stint before wintering in the Highlands from 17th December 1966 until 22nd April 1967 when it returned to Haymarket. For the period when this illustration was recorded, D5319 transferred to Inverness on 27th July 1967 but it was due to move south once again just weeks after it had completed this duty. Note that the Bo-Bo has retained its original livery - for now! *John Boyes (ARPT).*

On the following morning D5341 was working on the Speyside line and is seen leaving Craigellachie Junction, Banffshire with a somewhat heftier load. Note the livery change to Rail blue and the double arrow symbol which has replaced the BR crest. However, the D prefix has been retained albeit at one end only. Now where did that cab door, which has retained the green and white livery, come from? *John Boyes (ARPT).*

Another EE Type 4 at Newcastle Central, or rather waiting at the signal on the bypass lines on the southern edge of the station. Undated, the image shows D270 at the head of what was probably the meat train from Aberdeen to London. The Type 4 is new and clean – the last fact will become clearer because D270 was now a Gateshead engine – and this particular product of Vulcan Foundry was handed over to BR on 11th April 1960. So, with the acceptance period out of the way, we can probably date this picture to the last week of April, give or take a day. Note the little ladders on the front. Are you all keeping count as to which had them and when? Good. *I.S.Carr (ARPT).*   37

We've seen the Up train with unusual motive power, now here is the Down *THAMES-CLYDE EXPRESS* with the normal offering in the shape of a Holbeck 'Peak' which today is D28. As we can see it is running through a rather wet Kikby Stephen West (no change there either) on Saturday 22nd April 1967 when most of the local facilities were still intact, although a stone wall further along the platform has given-up-the-ghost, temporarily. *John Boyes (ARPT).*

This particular DBT was No.B964040E which was constructed at York carriage works in 1962 as part of Lot 3448, which covered 68 similar vehicles. When photographed at Newcastle Central in 1962 with Sulzer Type 2 D5097, it was allocated to Gateshead depot. Later in life this DBT transferred to the Western Region, working from Acton yard. *B.Anderson (ARPT).*

We venture into the Paint shop at Doncaster on Sunday 8th April 1962 and are greeted by BRC&W Type 2 D5382, and one of the latter batches of EE Type 4s (either D386, D387 or D388). It be noted by those following the door handle saga in previous volumes that D5382 has them clearly fitted half-way, immediately beneath the window sill. D5382 was bound for the LMR at Cricklewood but would not arrive at that place until Friday 20th of the month such was the thoroughness of the acceptance procedure which these locomotives underwent. It would have been useful to view one of the BR inspectors' reports issued after completion of one such Doncaster trial. I suppose they must have viewed the whole of the underside of these diesels too, if only to make sure that the paint had indeed been applied to all areas. In a pointless act of vandalism somebody, visiting as an enthusiast, apparently damaged the paintwork of one of the newly delivered diesel locomotives inside this shop which afterwards resulted in a complete ban on any visitors to the place! *George Watson.*

Let us revert back to 1961 and view one of Gateshead's first Type 5s, in fact their first Deltic acquisition. Looking surprisingly resplendent, the as yet to be named D9002 stands alongside the ruins of the steam roundhouses which at that time were being demolished, rebuilt, and fashioned into what was to become Gateshead diesel depot. However, the opening of that establishment was still some time off when D9002 was captured on film with a grotty looking EE Type 4 on the right, and the yard became the usual stabling point for the diesels with trips to Heaton for maintenance. The ground hereabouts, it will be noted, was made up mainly of coal dust with a mix of ashes and cinders; hardly the best environment for the complex – compared with steam locomotives – machines on which BR were pinning so much. *P.J.Robinson.*

This is what the 'Western's' did! Running wrong-line because of emergency works to the north, at Stoke Canon, D1044 WESTERN DUCHESS slows at Cowley Bridge signal box to enable the signal bobby to give instructions to the Secondman. The date is 4th July 1969, a Friday, and 42 the train is one of the inter-regional workings from the north-east; no doubt the first of many on this summer weekend. *John Boyes (ARPT).*

Gateshead based BR Sulzer Type 2 D5182 leads a funeral cortege past the steelworks at Cliff House, West Hartlepool on 9th September 1967 bound for York, and then onward transit from there to a scrapyard in Chesterfield. The unlucky duo of steam locomotives are Q6 No.63455, ex-Tyne Dock and condemned 22nd June; the 0-8-0 is accompanied by Peppercorn K1 No.62048, ex West Hartlepool, which was condemned on 19th June. Once their purchaser has done with them, the remains of the two steam locomotives would be packed into numerous 16-ton mineral wagons and then sent to a steel works near you; perhaps even this place, which would add a sense of irony to the whole exercise. More than likely the pair would end up at a number of different locations, the differing grades of metal requiring separate treatment. Note that no brake vans are attached but 'riders' would be present in the cabs of the condemned locomotives. *John Boyes (ARPT)*.

Another Type 2 involved with hauling a 'dead' steam locomotive around the North-East was BR Sulzer D5103 which, on a rather damp Friday, 4th October 1968, was photographed crossing the B1299 road as it headed through East Boldon station in the Sunderland direction. This particular train was no funeral cortege however because the Q6 in tow was none other than No.63395, the preserved example. On its way from Tyne Dock MPD to Thornaby MPD for preservation. D5103, which was one of the Darlington built examples, was renumbered 24103 in February 1974 but just over two years later it was withdrawn, aged twenty-six which, for a diesel locomotive, was pretty good going. East Boldon station was much older than both of the locomotives and is still operational as part of the Tyne & Wear system. *John Boyes (ARPT).*

London's Liverpool Street station. Saturday morning, 31st May 1958. Making an impressive sight, EE Type 4 D202 is at the head of a Great Eastern lines express. Barely a month old, the big diesel has already managed to accumulate a lot of road dirt around its bogies and lower body; Stratford's reputation for cleaning its locomotives was similar to that of Gateshead. Only three of the class had reached the east London depot by this date, although D203 and D204 were at Doncaster undergoing acceptance trials and would soon boost the small fleet so that full diesel working of the Norwich services especially could begin. *C.J.B.Sanderson (ARPT).*

45

This is Doncaster built 0-6-0DM D2071, on Sunday 19th August 1962, outstationed from Bradford Hammerton Street 56G to Mirfield 56D. Put into traffic on 13th October 1959, the locomotive is fitted with a vacuum ejector but only a three-link coupling instead of the screw coupling, the latter being ideal combination for working empty stock. However, Mirfield was fairly bereft of carriage siding so it would be goods yards and trip working for this diesel; perhaps even acting as shed pilot, moving coal wagons onto the stage, and other minor duties. Although part of the 0-6-0DM fleet which became TOPS Class 03, D2071 never made it to renumbering and was withdrawn in May 1972 after five years at Gateshead depot. It was one of the few diesel locomotives to be sold for scrap to Drapers of Hull who scrapped four of the class during November and December 1973. By coincidence, Drapers also managed to cut up four of the similar Class 04 at the earlier date of August 1968 when they were probably at their busiest taking apart hundreds of steam locomotives too. *C.J.B.Sanderson (ARPT).*

In *D for Diesels: 3*, we illustrated NBL Type 2 Bo-Bo DE D6120 passing through Newcastle in June 1959 en route from the makers in Glasgow to Doncaster for acceptance trials. We now present a scene from the 'gradual exodus' of the class away from London when they were all relocated (banished more like) to Scotland. Although the image is undated, the date would have been somewhere around 24th April 1960, which was the day for D6100 and D6101's departure from Hornsey to a new life north of the border. They have now reached Newcastle and, judging by their position at the west end of Central station, it is late afternoon/early evening and the pair are probably about to spend the night at Heaton shed although, with a crew change, the journey may well have continued because a fuel stop would not be necessary; the ER having gladly topped-up the tanks before the Type 2s left London. *Ian H.Hodgson (ARPT).*

47

Remember those British Railways exhibitions and Open days in the 60s' when the latest and greatest in BR traction was put on show for all and sundry. This is the Derby works open day of 29th August 1959 (the annual Flower Show to give it the proper title) with D2 HELVELLYN having pride of place alongside the works offices. Note that the cab – at this end of the locomotive anyway – is bereft of members of the public or anyone else; the authorities were keen to have the general public look but not touch. After all, most BR footplatemen had yet to enter the cab of a diesel and have a fiddle with the controls. For the record, other locomotives on show included: D3782, D5021, 'Britannia' No.70004 WILLIAM SHAKESPEARE, and BR Standard Cl.9F No.92165. *Ian H.Hodgson (ARPT)*.

(*above*) Gateshead based EE Type 4 D249 waits for the signals on the by-pass lines at Newcastle (Central) in 1964 before proceeding over the Tyne and home. This is one of the class still equipped at this late date with those small ladders on the nose. (*below*) On the same day at Newcastle Central's platform 8, Brush Type 4 D1528 also awaits the signal with an Up express. *Both B.Anderson (ARPT).*

BRC&W Type 3 D6542 heads a Down passenger service (112) at Ashford at an unknown date in the mid '60s. Unlike their smaller Type 2 cousins on the ER, LMR and ScR, the SR Bo-Bos had their numbers positioned firmly half way down the cab side sheet, well away from the mid-drift band to which the Type 2 number groups seem to be virtually attached. What the whole exercise proved was that each region certainly did have its own way on the various details in the designs, even on those locomotives which had a likeness from the same manufacturer. The SR realised early on, for instance, that connecting doors between locomotives were not required so their Type 3 was 'clean' and smooth at the ends compared with the main line locomotives on most of the other regions. *Ian H.Hodgson (ARPT).*

(*above*) Dairycoates new acquisition D6740 spent the weekend of 18th and 19th August 1962 at Normanton shed. Some two and a half months old, its upper body retains some of that factory freshness. (*below*) Darnall's D6807 was at Retford on Sunday 7th July 1963 and was looking as smart – above the bogies – as when it left Vulcan Foundry six months previously. *Both C.J.B.Sanderson (ARPT).*

We haven't presented any diesel shunters at Colwick before in this series so to make amends we have this nice illustration of Barclay D2403 on the shed yard on Friday 12th July 1963. Having arrived at Colwick on 29th June 1963, the 0-6-0DM was only visiting the depot on a 'suitability loan' from Boston and actually returned home on the last day of the following October (not a bad stint for a loan). Some compatibility must have been found between Colwick and the diesel shunters because in the first week of the following January D2403 returned to the Nottingham depot and brought sisters D2401, D2402, D2407, and D2409 along. And so began an eighteen month relationship between Colwick and the Barclays. On 24th July 1965 the five Colwick examples (half of the class) moved on to Barrow Hill (see D for Diesels Vol.2). It was actually a sunny day when this scene was recorded but the inevitable overcast from Colwick Loco. won the day in the lighting stakes. *C.J.B.Sanderson (ARPT)*.

Let's have a look at a couple of BR 350 h.p. 0-6-0DE shunters for a change. (*above*) D3485 rests at its home shed New England on Saturday 13th July 1963. (*below*) Likewise, D3491 is switched-off for the weekend at March depot on the same Saturday. *Both C.J.B.Sanderson (ARPT).*

Still at March on Saturday 13th July 1963, we have a couple of 'traffic cone' Drewry 0-6-0s from different eras, and makers, to compare. The first things that leap out are the different number fonts and sizes; cab windows and doors; cab roofs – style and shape; bonnet heights; couplings and vacuum pipe stands; steps on the radiator housing, etc., etc. (*above*) D2030 is one of the Swindon lot from October 1958 whilst D2240 (*left*) stems from the slightly earlier era of Vulcan Foundry in June 1956. There wasn't a lot in it age-wise, nor internally with the same engine, drive, horsepower, etc., but the changes in detail were phenomenal. Oh, don't forget the wheel diameter. Once again evolution at work! *Both C.J.B.Sanderson (ARPT).*

After exposure given to the prototype Deltic in the last D for Diesels, we thought that one more offering would not seen too pushy. Here at Welwyn (North) on the afternoon of Friday 19th August 1960, the big diesel roars through the wayside station with a King's Cross bound express. I hope the photographer was aware of a northbound train approaching from behind! *D.J.Dippie.*

Couldn't resist this one at Bletchley, in the summer of 1959. The Up service of *THE MERSEYSIDE EXPRESS* is about to make the ground shake. *J.Archer (ARPT)*.

(*above*) The simple side of E.D.1 at Newton Heath shed on Saturday 29th August 1959. *N.W.Skinner (ARPT)*. (*below*) The complicated side – for modellers – with what looks like 'add-ons' or retro fittings but were already attached as per factory finish when the little 0-4-0DM went into traffic. Although in this view the locomotive was captured in virtually the same spot as the upper illustration, the two images were recorded three years apart because the date of this picture is 8th August 1956, a Wednesday. It was the only diesel on shed on this date and when it visited 26A for maintenance from its usual haunt at Castleton Permanent Way depot, that situation would remain so for a number of years thereafter. The complimentary chimney would do justice to any little steam locomotive engaged on similar duties. *F.W.Hampson (ARPT)*.

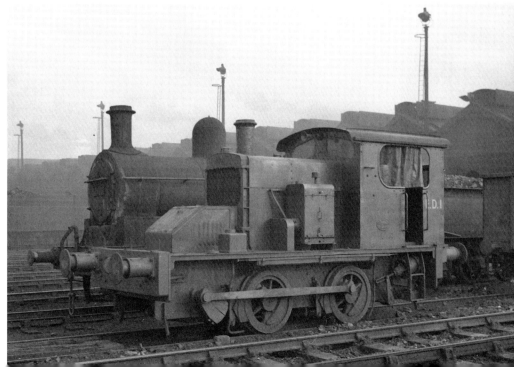

Shildon, Friday 8th August 1958, with Drewry D2316 working the yard along with an unidentified sister engine. We are looking towards Shildon station, with the line to Bishop Auckland branching off to the right. Dead ahead is the line to the wagon works. Behind the cameraman was another yard. Except for the station, and the lines to the north-west, everything has gone although the NRM's annexe known as Locomotion is located immediately behind the camera. *I.S.Carr (ARPT).*

A nice bit of nostalgia in more ways than one. **D1035 WESTERN TROOPER** runs through Totnes over the fast lines en route for Plymouth with an express on 23rd May 1969. Over on the left, in the siding are six-wheel glass-lined milk tankers waiting for the motive power which would take them to London or somewhere near the capital where their contents could be pumped into other fixed tanks which would in turn fill literally millions of bottles of milk – every day! That was until BR lost the contract to transport milk from the West Country, West Wales, and the North-West of England, indeed from anywhere it was produced, on a daily basis in dedicated trains of milk tanks or in passenger trains with tanks attached. In the background is the Unigate Dairy or creamery as they like to call them in Devon. You can hear the bottles rattlin'. So, lots here to digest and its no use crying over spilt milk! *John Boyes (ARPT).*

With pictures of steam/diesel combinations erring towards scarce on the scale of what is available, we present this nice study of EE Type 4 D250 and Gresley A3 No.60065 KNIGHT OF THISTLE hauling a diverted Up ECML express at Portobello Lane, Sunderland on Sunday 7th May 1961. *D.J.Dippie.*

D1069 WESTERN VANGUARD stands at the north end of Plymouth station on a date which could have been any time from 1961 to 1977. In fact it was 27th May 1975, perhaps given away by the TOPS panel beneath the cast numberplate, and the self adhesive LA badge above. The driver is having a quiet smoke prior to departure and just below his elbow is a bracket for one of the name plaques on which BR wanted their drivers to display their name. It was a scheme which was doomed from the start because in steam days BR had tried the self same idea on all regions and it was rejected outright - BR footplatemen had long memories and old habits take a long time to die out. *T.Ermel.*   61

Nearly brand new or so it would seem! D261 at Haymarket depot on 28th July 1961 looking for all the world as though it had recently arrived from the makers. So, what had really happened? It had either had an exceptional, and I mean exceptional clean, or it had just returned from shops where a coat of paint had been skilfully applied. But then the latter explanation begs the question – why? Looks nice though! This was Haymarket's second new EE Type 4 which they received in late February 1960 (D260-D266) to accompany the four second-hand but in fact only a week or so old examples (D256-D259) which arrived from York in mid-February. *D.J.Dippie.*

'Built 1964 Swindon' the worksplate states. Why? Just over a year old and D9500 stands idle alongside the main line at Bath Road depot in Bristol on 19th September 1965. Admitted, it was a Sunday morning but come Monday and the operating staff would be wondering how to best utilise the 0-6-0 diesel-hydraulic Type 1 when there was basically nothing for it to do. This class of locomotive really summed up what was wrong with British Railways and in particular the Western Region at the time. The WR was allowed to build these locomotives during the period when they and all the other regions of BR were losing goods traffic to road haulage at an alarming rate. Goods yards were closing down and the kind of traffic these 0-6-0DHs were designed to handle had virtually disappeared, even then! That the WR was given carte blanche freedom to choose, design and then build what locomotives they thought they needed was nothing short madness in an organisation which was basically bankrupt, in every sense. Waste was endemic! Even the shedplate carried by D9500 was different from the standard fixture in that it had the alpha suffix in front of the area code number – A82 – rather than the other way round – 82A. On the last day of 1947 a group of men got together and decreed that they were not going to comply with the new regime which took over their world at midnight. They appear to have kept that pact going, at what cost to the taxpayer, until they left the organisation as individuals. Ironically, two other nationalised industries purchased many of these locomotives as soon as they were withdrawn by BR and appear to have got their money's worth out of them - what they actually paid is unknown but it would have been nothing like the original cost of 1964. *K.Groundwater (ARPT).*

Stratford depot, 22nd May 1965, with two more likely candidates for dodgy purchases of the decade: the BTH Type 1 (*above*) and the NBL Type 1 (*below*). D8409 represents the latter design; luckily BR only bought ten of them during the summer of 1958. Ten years later they were all withdrawn and sold for scrap. D8240 looks aesthetically more pleasing and that may well have had an influence of the larger numbers acquired by BR between November 1957 and February 1961 when forty-four of their kind were put into traffic. They too were being withdrawn by 1968 but it was 1971 before they had finally been eliminated. *Both K.Groundwater (ARPT).*

Yet another Anglo-Scottish working but this time its a non-revenue movement. EE Type 1s D8081 and D8082, we are accurately informed, were recorded heading through Newcastle (Central) on Friday 1st September 1961 en route for Glasgow from the Robert Stephenson & Hawthorn factory at Darlington. (see also page 66 in Vol.3). The Friday release to BR was typical English Electric practice be it from the Darlington plant or the factory at Newton-le-Willows. *I.S.Carr (ARPT).*

Far from home? Not really in the great scheme of things. Bristol Bath Road's Brush Type 4 D1675 AMAZON rests at Darlington shed in 1966 after arriving in the north-east with a working from deep within the Western Region. Only about a year old at this stage of its life, the Crewe-built Co-Co had been named in November 1965 and was one of sixteen of the WR allocated locomotives named during 1965 and 1966. D1675 and the location depicted here embodied the standardisation and 'go anywhere' policy which BR created for their motive power. What became Class 47 was a class of locomotive which could be found nearly everywhere on British Railways, doing anything: Margate, on an excursion from the West Midlands perhaps; Holyhead, on a boat train from Euston; Penzance, on a sleeper from London; Didcot on a coal train from Nottinghamshire; Teesside on a train of steel empties from South Wales; Inverness on an overnight passenger working from England. The list is endless and is testimony that BR got some things right regarding their choice of locomotive types. However, it was not all plain sailing at first with this class but that's another story. Now then, what is that vehicle-less buffer doing on the ground? *V.Wake (ARPT).*

It would appear that Hunslet 0-4-0DM D2950 was off to the knackers yard but this little diesel was far from finished when it was photographed on a Flatrol wagon at Dairycoates on Christmas Eve 1966. It was in fact in transit from Ipswich to Goole (transfer date 23rd December 1966) and had been brought to Hull where facilities for its removal from the bogie wagon were available. To keep the diesel within the loading gauge whilst in transit, the upper portion of the cab has been removed but that piece of kit would be re-united with the locomotive once the 0-4-0 was back on the rails at Dairycoates shed. A quick transit to Goole shed afterwards would see it performing for a further twelve months before it was sold off to private industry after withdrawal on 30th December 1967. Starting life at Ipswich on 3rd December 1954 as No.11500, the diesel-mechanical was renumbered in April 1958. For the record, D2950 had two sisters, D2951 and D2952, which were also allocated to Ipswich. D2951 joined D2950 at Goole shortly after this scene was recorded and similarly went on working for BR until the end of 1967. The final member of the trio, D2952, was however withdrawn on Christmas Day 1966, probably at Hull after undergoing a similar journey to the other two. Although Ipswich is recorded as its last depot, and it most certainly was, it does not necessarily mean that the withdrawal was carried out there. In all eventuality, 32B would have wanted to remove the un-required locomotive from their premises and would not condemn it prior to its transit north. D2952 eventually ended up at a scrapyard in Rotherham by August 1967. During their time at Ipswich the trio were required to wear skirts and cowcatchers on account of them working over public roads but in this view neither skirts, cowcatchers nor shunters steps are fitted; the latter would be refitted with the cab but the other two unwanted items were discarded. *K.Gregory (ARPT).*

The Tyne Dock-Consett iron ore trains were still steam hauled in 1964 but the banking duties were undertaken by either steam or diesel locomotives. In this illustration at Annfield East on a sunny evening in the summer of 64' the banking was undertaken by a combination of English Electric power with a Type 4 next to the train, with a Type 3 trailing with DBT and brakevan. With about 500 tons of ore in the bogie wagons, the BR Standard 9F leading the formation does not seem to be overly taxed by the nine-wagon 750 ton train even though the gradient is still a mean 1 in 53 – it had just eased from 1 in 35 according to the gradient post – so perhaps the diesels were throwing some weight behind their efforts. It was normal for the steam hauled iron ore trains to stop at South Pelaw to attach (actually couple) a banking engine, because it was from that location where the gradients started to become steeper than the 1 in 135 maximum experienced during the journey from Tyne Dock (approx. 30 feet above sea level) to South Pelaw. There is a slight ascent of 1 in 60 from the loading dock to the South Shields-Newcastle line when the 9F and its heavy train get rear-end assistance from a diesel shunter prior to crossing the electrified route and proceeding westwards and upwards on the 28-mile journey. Besides the curvature apparent here at Annfield East, the gradient got as steep at 1 in 31 for short stretches of the climb to Consett (approx. 900 feet above sea level). Soon, the banking engines would detach from the train but rather than run back to South Pelaw 'light engine' these two were proceeding to Consett to pick up their own train. *P.J.Robinson.*

ACCIDENTS – LARGE & SMALL

The rather battered remains of Brush D1671 rest in the scrapyard of R.S.Hayes at Bridgend on 23rd August 1966 awaiting attention from the cutters. The Type 4 had been derailed by a landslip near Bridgend in mid-December 1965 and was immediately afterwards hit head-on by EE Type 3 D6983 working in the opposite direction. Both locomotives were so badly damaged they were subsequently withdrawn. After salvageable parts had been recovered by BR, the hulks were then sold for scrap to the same private yard. This was the first Class 47 to be withdrawn. Carrying the name THOR at the time of the accident, the nameplate was transferred from D1671 to D1677. *K.Gregory (ARPT).*

These are a couple of views of DP2 after it had been in collision with a derailed wagon on the ECML at Cod Beck, south of Thirsk on the afternoon of Thursday 31st August 1967. Just over three hours into its journey, DP2 was heading the midday King's Cross to Edinburgh express (1A26 comprised thirteen well filled coaches) along the Down fast line when it struck the 23rd wagon of the loaded twenty-six wagon Cliffe to Uddingston cement train – travelling on the Down slow – which had itself just become derailed because of a defective wagon. Only the one wagon actually ended up fouling the Down fast line; the cement train had parted between the 11th and 12th wagons (this 12th wagon LA233, was the culprit) and along with the goods train locomotive (D283), the first eleven vehicles had remained on the track, travelling on for a further quarter of a mile or so before being able to stop. Wagons 13 to 20 had careered down the embankment whilst those from 21 onwards had derailed but stayed on the formation of the four-track main line. When the driver of the northbound express, which was travelling at 80 m.p.h. behind the stricken goods train, saw in the distance (some 600 yards) the resultant dust cloud caused by the derailment, he immediately stopped accelerating and, when he realised that one of the wagons was across his path, he braked heavily and shut down DP2's engine thinking of the possible fire hazard if the wagon was carrying petroleum products. When the collision took place the passenger train was travelling at a much reduced 50 m.p.h. but nevertheless seven passengers sadly lost their lives whilst another forty-five were injured, some quite seriously, as the heavy cement laden wagon (LA264) ripped into the side of the passenger rolling stock. Meanwhile, the goods train driver had gone back to the telephone on the signal post which he had just passed with his heavily braking locomotive and informed the signalman at Thirsk of his trains' dilemma. The signalman immediately put all signals on either side of the incident to danger, but then that same driver witnessed the resultant collision between the express and the stranded wagon. Luckily, a southbound express, which was just approaching Thirsk at speed when the signals were put to danger, was stopped at the station otherwise it may have hit the derailed Down express, which was by now fouling the Up fast line, with perhaps even greater loss of life. The weather was clear and dry but nevertheless the combination of speed and bad luck could not alter the inevitable incident involving the Down express. DP2 never recovered from the accident and the severe damage is evident in these two views although the bent main frame of the locomotive cannot be detected from these angles. Both the driver and secondman of DP2 were fortunate not to receive any injury. Seven of the passenger vehicles were also damaged and derailed. The cause was put down to excessive wear on the suspension of wagon LA223 caused by the ingestion of and resultant corrosion of cement dust. The four wheel wagon was actually travelling just below the maximum permitted speed (45 m.p.h.) for that type of vehicle at the time of the incident. Speed limits were further imposed on the wagons after the accident to 35 m.p.h. for loaded wagons and 50 when empty. DP2 was broken up in 1970. *Both John Boyes (ARPT).*

To finish on a somewhat lighter note, we present Sulzer Type 2 D5106 in the future. The 'D' prefix has been abolished, boring blue became the chosen livery, gangway doors had been either welded up or replaced, and every thing appeared to be going pear-shaped, especially in Clackheugh. The date is 15th August 1972 and the Bo-Bo is well and truly stuck between the rails. Re-railing would be a simple enough job with the correct equipment so, having realised their predicament was hopeless without assistance (they had tried some pieces of timber but to no avail), the crew take a walk. 'I hate Tuesday's!' *I.S.Carr (ARPT)*